READY, SET, BUILD YOUR BRAND

A 21-STEP GUIDE TO ASSIST WITH BUILDING YOUR BRAND

DR. SYNOVIA DOVER-HARRIS

Ready, Set, Build Your Brand. A 21-step guide to assist with building your brand

First Printing
ISBN **978-1-943284-14-6**(pbk.)
ISBN **978-1-943284-15-3**(ebk)

A2Z Books, LLC
Lithonia, GA 30058
www.A2ZBooksPublishing.com
Manufactured in the United States of America
A2Z Books Publishing has allowed this work to remain exactly as the author intended, verbatim.

INTRODUCTION

It's 7:30 am, and this is my 4th project today already. I am what most would consider a serial entrepreneur because I have a number of companies. I currently own a business and branding consulting/coaching firm, a publishing company that also prints commercially, I am partners in an accessories/lifestyle brand, and I co-own a gym. So on any given morning, day or night, I am constantly looking for ways to market my companies and build my brands, as I am today while starting to write this book.

When I started my first real company over 15 years ago (because I had many before that), I never took the time to do that. I merely created products and services and automatically assumed they would sell with no brand building and little marketing efforts. "Boy was I wrong;" one of my previous business partners and I created this workshop about 6 or 7 years ago where we taught individuals how to write a book. It was called writing for a purpose, and we thought we had hit the jackpot because not a lot of people were showing individuals how to write a book (unlike today where it is taught on every corner and webinar how to write or publish a book). We marketed the workshops on our social media sites and used what little resources we had, but we could never get a full house.

We wracked our brains for years trying to figure out what we were doing wrong and all of a sudden it hit me that although we were going out there and offering this information and sometimes even for free, we still didn't get a lot of traction because an effective brand had not been built. We both should have known better, but we were so busy watching other people's workshops, and events sell out that we just thought it was something easy to do. Most people who have companies do not know

1

how to build successful brands because building a brand is much more than creating a logo and a website.

Hi, I'm Dr. Synovia Dover-Harris, and I am going to give you the tools you need to start building that powerhouse Company and setting yourself apart from your get your competitors with these 21 Steps in Ready, Set Build Your Brand. The most important step in building your brand is getting started....

HOW TO USE THIS GUIDE

This guide contains 21 Steps to Building your Brand. All of the steps are action items that you will need to complete and will assist you with the Brand Building Process. This book can be utilized to brand any company as well as individuals who have personal brands. Most of the steps should be easy to complete and implement, however, because this is a resource guide assistance, may be required.

You will need:
- An allocated place to work.
- At least 30-45 minutes to complete each step (some may require more, and others may require less).
- A computer or cell phone (to conduct research).
- Something to write on (notebook/journal).
- Something to write with (pen/pencil).
- A calendar or scheduling system of some sort to create timelines/deadlines.

The steps/action items are strategically designed to align and propel you in the right direction to building your brand.

READY…

SET...

BUILD YOUR BRAND!

CONTENTS

Step 1
Brand Identity

Step 1 is identifying your brand. A business brand identity is how the company wants to be perceived by their customers.

Identifying your brand is vital because you have to know who you are to determine where you are going.

Take the next 30 minutes and Research Band Identity …

Determine what type of brand you are; for example:
- ✓ A Luxury Brand.
- ✓ A Product or Service Brand.
- ✓ A Value Brand.
- ✓ A Lifestyle Brand.
- ✓ An Organic.
- ✓ An Ethical Brand.

You can identify your Brand by answering the following:
- ✓ Who are you?
- ✓ What do you want to be known for?
- ✓ What are your company's purpose, value, and unique value proposition?

What type of brand are you and what is your purpose?

For example; A2Z Books, LLC is a product and service business brand. I want to be known as the company to go for all branding and publishing needs. A2Z Books, LLC is Publishing and Branding Consulting Firm that offers innovative business, branding and publishing products and services created for businesses, business professionals, entrepreneurs, educators, and artists.

Identify your Brand.

USE THIS AREA TO WRITE
ABOUT YOUR BRAND

_____

_____

_____

_____

_____

_____

_____

_____

_____

_____

_____

_____

_____

_____

_____

_____

_____

_____

_____

_____

_____

_____

_____

Step 2
Brand Target Market

Step 2 is determining your Brand's Target Market. A Target market is the group of consumers the brand will aim its marketing efforts toward.

Take the next 30 minutes and Research Target Market …

Your Brand's Target Market is determined by answering who will want your products and/or services through the following questions:

- ✓ Who is your customer (Men, Women, Companies, etc.)?
- ✓ What do they look like (18-25, 60 & up, African, Americans or Small Start-up companies)?
- ✓ What do they do (College students, retired, & sell products)?
- ✓ Where can we find them (Universities, retirement homes, & Instagram)?
- ✓ What is their education level?
- ✓ What is their income level?
- ✓ What is there Marital & Family Status?

After you have answered these, you will know who you are targeting with your brand and where you can find them and how. You do not want to spend marketing efforts, time, and money and market to someone that is not your target market. Also by determining your brand's target market, you will know how to create your branding strategies.

Who is your Brand's Target Market?

USE THIS AREA TO WRITE
ABOUT YOUR BRAND

_____

_____

_____

_____

_____

_____

_____

_____

_____

_____

_____

_____

_____

_____

Step 3
Brand Strategies

Step 3 is creating a branding strategy. The Branding Strategy is created by setting Branding goals and then creating the steps to accomplish these goals.

Take the next 30 minutes and Research Branding Strategies …

Answer the following:

- ✓ What will my customers think when they think about this brand?
- ✓ What are my guiding principles?
- ✓ What are my brand's mission and vision?
- ✓ Is my brand credible?

Now ask yourself:

- ✓ What sets my brand apart from others?
- ✓ Who is my brand's target audience?
- ✓ What do I want to accomplish as a brand?
- ✓ How will I Accomplish these branding goals?

For example: I want to be the top publishing and branding firm in the south-east that is dedicated to startups and first-time authors. I will accomplish these goals by ensuring my products and services are effective and efficient and are offered at a good rate. I will enlist the help of a marketing and branding firm to help me accomplish this goal. I know that my company's value and purpose is to assist, so, therefore, a branding strategy will be hiring consultants who are educated, well versed in these areas, and professional.

Create your Branding Strategies!

USE THIS AREA TO WRITE
ABOUT YOUR BRAND

_____

_____

_____

_____

_____

_____

_____

_____

_____

_____

_____

_____

_____

_____

_____

_____

_____

_____

_____

_____

_____

_____

_____

_____

_____

_____

Step 4
Brand Message

Step 4 is identifying your Brand's message, which is also known as your Brand's voice. Your brand message will explain to your consumers why you are in business in the first place as well as explain to the world what you do and how it is speaking for you.

Take the next 30 minutes and Research a Brand's Message/Voice …

Brand messages come in many forms and include things like:
- ✓ The Sale pitch.
- ✓ The Colors chosen.
- ✓ The Logos as well as the taglines and slogan.

Have you ever looked at someone's company and wondered what do they do? If you answered yes, this means their Brand message is unclear.

Here are some Tips to creating a Brand Message:
- ✓ Create an outline.
- ✓ Test the reaction of others.
- ✓ Make sure your message is:
  - ○ Clear,
  - ○ Consistent, and
  - ○ Competitive.

Nike's Brand Message is "Just Do It" - Meaning to get it done as an athlete. Apple's Brand Message is "Think Different" because they want you to be innovative when utilizing their products.

What is your Brand's Message?

USE THIS AREA TO WRITE
ABOUT YOUR BRAND

_____

_____

_____

_____

_____

_____

_____

_____

_____

_____

_____

_____

_____

_____

_____

_____

_____

_____

_____

_____

_____

_____

_____

_____

_____

_____

_____

Step 5
Brand Image

Step 5 is creating and identifying your Brand's image. A Brand's image is created through visuals and intertwines with the brand's message and can be seen in the company's logo. A Brand's image is a set of beliefs and what will attract and retain customers. Consumer's buy what a brand represents more than what the brand is, and as a result, identifying the brand's image is crucial.

Take the next 30 minutes and Research a Brand's Image ...

The Brand's Image is also:
- ✓ What the consumer will think about internally when they think about your brand.
- ✓ The Consumer's Perception.
- ✓ The Impression.
- ✓ The Look.
- ✓ Organic.

And should reflect:
- ✓ Positivity.
- ✓ The Brand's persona.

Answer the following to identify your Brand's image:
- ✓ What will I include in my imagery (marketing, social media, & packaging) to ensure our personality is reflected? (Our Business logo).
- ✓ How do I want to be perceived by my consumer? (Fun & Innovative).
- ✓ What strategies and techniques will I use to assist with solidifying my brand's image? (Creativity, Consistency, Professionalism).

What is your Brand's Image?

USE THIS AREA TO WRITE
ABOUT YOUR BRAND

_____

_____

_____

_____

_____

_____

_____

_____

_____

_____

_____

_____

_____

Step 6
Brand Equity

Step 6 is acquiring Brand Equity. "Equity is defined as the value or worth of something." Brand equity is the value of a brand in the marketplace.

Take the next 30 minutes and Research a Brand's Equity …

Having worth and value in your Brand is important because no one wants to have a brand that is not looked upon as valuable or worth anything.

Can you think of a company who has Good Brand Equity?

Now, think of a company that has Bad Brand Equity?

Good brand equity is associated with well-known companies. For example: Mercedes Benz or Honda and bad brand equity is associated with companies that are no longer around or are on their way out. For example: Blockbuster and Daewoo.

The way to ensure you have Brand Equity is to:

✓ Remain innovative.

✓ Solve a Problem.

✓ Provide a superior product/service and make sure you do it better than anyone else.

✓ Make sure your brand's message is clear.

Note: A well-known brand name is more valuable than the product itself because people buy what they think more often than what they know.

How will you obtain your Brand's Equity?

USE THIS AREA TO WRITE
ABOUT YOUR BRAND

_____

_____

_____

_____

_____

_____

_____

_____

_____

_____

_____

_____

_____

Step 7
Brand Demand

Step 7 is creating Brand Demand. The Brand's Demand is the request of your products and services. Having a demand for your brand is crucial and is what is required for a brand to grow on a continuous basis.

Take the next 30 minutes and Research a Brand's Demand …

Can you think of Brand that is in High Demand?

One brand that I know that is in high demand is Chick Fil A. I know this because whenever I go to Chick Fil A, no matter what time of day it is, the line is always wrapped around the building. We all would like to have this type of demand, but we also know it can take years for a brand like this to be built, therefore it may take years for your products and services to be demanded, but it is doable.

The first step in creating a brand's demand is research. Interviews and surveys should be conducted, and you will find out:

✓ What your customers want and how much?

✓ What will they pay for it?

✓ Who has it already?

✓ What can you do to create a competitive advantage?

As a Brand, you have to provide something that your consumers feel like they cannot live without.

Here are 3 ways to create a demand for your product:

✓ Be Unique.

✓ Offer something better than the competition.

✓ Make consumers feel important.

How will you obtain your Brand's Demand?

USE THIS AREA TO WRITE
ABOUT YOUR BRAND

_____

_____

_____

_____

_____

_____

_____

_____

_____

_____

_____

_____

_____

_____

_____

_____

_____

_____

_____

_____

_____

_____

_____

_____

_____

Step 8
Branding Process

Step 8 is creating your Brand's Process. A Brand's process is the way your business will be running and is a structure of activities.

Take the next 30 minutes and Research a Business Process …

Every brand needs a bulletproof process of how the business will be operated that connects with the brand's values. However, most entrepreneurs' especially new businesses have trouble creating processes.

Processes need to be set up for Consistency and Cohesiveness.

I am an avid coffee drinker, and I like Starbucks, but I LOVE Dunkin Doughnuts Caramel or Butter Pecan Ice Coffee. Dunkin Doughnuts branding processes have been mastered because as long as I have been going there, my coffee always tastes the same, the greeting and overall professionalism are usually the same, and even the way they speak to you in the drive-thru is consistent.

Creating a brand process is of particular importance because consistency and cohesiveness are two vital components of making a brand great and automation makes a brand.

Processes include things like:

- ✓ How your products and services will be delivered.
- ✓ How you will answer the phones and email.
- ✓ How often you will put out new products etc.
- ✓ How you will accept payments.
- ✓ How you deliver customer service.

What are my Brand's processes?

USE THIS AREA TO WRITE
ABOUT YOUR BRAND

_____

_____

_____

_____

_____

_____

_____

_____

_____

_____

_____

_____

_____

Step 9
Brand Communication

Step 9 is creating the Brand's communications. A successful brand cannot exist without a proper communication strategy.

Take the next 30 minutes and Research Communication Strategies ...

Your Brand's Communications are the type of content you provide on social media, blogs & websites, emails, printed materials, and involves when and how an event is planned.

Communication is different from marketing because the brand's communication is the exchanging of information, whereas, the brand's marketing is the activities that involve making consumers aware of the brand and although the two definitely intertwined, they are vastly different.

Communication is what is delivered, and marketing is how it is delivered. Communication is focused on what and marketing is focused on who.

Your Brand Communications speaks on your Brand's Message and should:

✓ Highlight the Brand.
✓ Be informative.
✓ Show the company's personality.
✓ Be Focused.
✓ Be Thoughtful.
✓ Be Unique.
✓ Be Purposeful.

What Brand Communications will you provide?

USE THIS AREA TO WRITE
ABOUT YOUR BRAND

_____

_____

_____

_____

_____

_____

_____

_____

_____

_____

_____

_____

_____

Step 10
Brand Marketing

Step 10 is creating the brand's marketing strategy and commercialization plan. Marketing is the events that include making consumers aware of the product and services of a brand. Marketing is one of the most important things a brand can do and is especially important for a new brand that many people do not know about.

Take the next 30 minutes and Research Marketing Strategies …

A well-executed marketing plan promotes brand awareness, brand identity, a brand demand, and brand loyalty, which converts to the brand's stream of income.

A Brand Markets through; Advertising, Communications, Social Media, and Promotions.

A Brand Marketing Strategy can be completed by:

- ✓ Identifying your target market (completed in Step 2).
- ✓ Identifying your Unique Value Proposition.
- ✓ Identifying the benefits of your product/service.
- ✓ Identifying your marketing budget based on how you want to market.
- ✓ Identifying the avenues you will market for example:
  - ○ Flyers,
  - ○ Social Media,
  - ○ Direct Mail/Emails
  - ○ Events, and
  - ○ Partnership etc.

What is your Brand's Marketing Strategy?

USE THIS AREA TO WRITE
ABOUT YOUR BRAND

_____

_____

_____

_____

_____

_____

_____

_____

_____

_____

_____

_____

_____

_____

_____

_____

_____

_____

_____

_____

_____

_____

_____

_____

_____

_____

Step 11
Brand Pricing

Step 11 is creating your Brand's Pricing Strategy. The way you price your products and services is one of the ultimate ways to identify a Brand's Roles in the marketplace.

Take the next 30 minutes and Research Pricing Strategies …

A brand's pricing is just as important as a brand's logo or a brand name because the price of a product and/or service determines how a brand is viewed. When prices are inexpensive, consumers may think the product is cheap and not good and when prices are expensive, consumers usually believe that a product is of better quality.

A pricing strategy is the actions that are taken to find the ideal price for a product or service and includes the competition price, distribution and production costs, the demand for the product as well as the economy. Additionally, the pricing strategy also assists with the maximization of profits.

There are 6 pricing strategies that a company can utilize to determine a price. Research and pick one for your company;

- ✓ Pricing at a Premium,
- ✓ Pricing for Market Penetration,
- ✓ Economy Pricing,
- ✓ Psychology Pricing, and
- ✓ Bundle Pricing.

What Brand Pricing Strategy will you use and why?

USE THIS AREA TO WRITE
ABOUT YOUR BRAND

_____

_____

_____

_____

_____

_____

_____

_____

_____

_____

_____

_____

_____

_____

_____

_____

_____

_____

_____

_____

_____

_____

_____

_____

_____

Step 12
Brand Packaging

Step 12 is identifying your brand's packaging. Brand Packaging is very important whether you are selling a product or service. As a matter of fact, if your product or service is not properly packaged, there is a chance that your potential customer or consumer may never even get the opportunity to experience what it is that you are selling because of unappealing packaging. They will walk or click right pass your brand.

Take the next 30 minutes and Research Packaging …

Bad packaging can turn the potential client off as well as fail to highlight what it is that you are selling. Remember that terms never judge a book by its cover, well your products and services will definitely be prejudged by your packaging, so, and that does not apply here.

You can be selling the best cupcakes in town, and no one would believe it if your packaging is subpar. If you are trying to do a business and build a brand with this cupcake, then investing in proper packaging is vital. Think of the Tiffany blue box and how the box itself has become more iconic than the actual gift in the product. 95% of new products fail because of the packaging. Remember packaging is powerful and packaging is the #1 Brand Builder. In fact, your packaging will sell your product faster than your product will sell your product.

Follow these five steps when creating your packaging:
- ✓ Be creative & unique (DO NOT copy another brand).
- ✓ Be visually appealing (Use vibrant colors & fonts).
- ✓ Be Simple (To read, to open, & to understand products message).
- ✓ Know your demographic (chose colors an image for your target).
- ✓ Make the end user experience something they will not forget.

What Brand Packaging are you using?

Step 13
Brand Placement

Step 13 is identifying where to place your Brand/Product. Brand placement also known as product placement goes hand in hand with the marketing of the brand. However, brand placement digs a little deeper into where the promotion and products should be placed for the consumer to see it and have the opportunity to consume or develop the desire to consume.

Take the next 30 minutes and Research Brand/Product Placement...

Have you ever wondered why certain products are sold and marketed certain places, and doesn't make any sense? That is because the owner of these companies did not take the time to research where they should place their brands before placing it.

I remember going to the festival of lights, and a vendor was giving away Italian ice. Now giving away free products is terrific to market. However, it was not the right place, since it was the middle of the winter. People were cold, and everyone would have much rather have free hot chocolate or hot coffee, which would have been a terrific time to place that brand. Therefore, a company that sold hot beverages would have done better branding there.

Some brands are better marketed at movie theaters, while another brand should be marketed online. Some brands can do very well at both and others struggle to find their place in the market.

When thinking of where to place your brand or product for more exposure research who might want your product/service (target market) and then determine where they shop and would see your promotional advances and place your ads or products there.

Where will you place your Brand?

Branding Tip: Put Your Logo and Slogan on anything you can give away.

USE THIS AREA TO WRITE
ABOUT YOUR BRAND

Step 14
Creating Brand Loyalty

Step 14 is creating brand loyalty. On Step 7, we determined how to build a brand demand, and today we will determine how to create brand loyalty. Brand loyalty is the magnitude of the devotion, faithfulness, and reliability of customers to a specific brand, which is usually expressed through repeated purchases.

Take the next 30 minutes and Research Brand Loyalty ...

Companies that spend a lot of time, money and effort building their brand usually do so, so that they can acquire the brand loyalty that keeps most companies in business. Sure, first time consumers are always great, but there is nothing better than knowing even before you launch a new product that you can instantly sell out because of the loyal fans that will buy no matter what the brand produces.

We all know about the loyalty of the Apple products, where people would stand in line for hours before the new iPhone is launched, or the loyalty to the Jordan Empire who at times has sold out sneakers in a matter of minutes. Also, loyalty can be built to service businesses as well. I am a loyal consumer of the woman (Kim) that does my eyebrows. Kim has arched my eyebrows for over 11 years, and no matter how good others are, I will not go anywhere. I am a loyal fan of her and the brand she has built.

Most companies dream of building this type of loyalty and here are three easy steps that will assist you with building brand loyalty with your consumers:

✓ Connect with your customers on an intimate level.
✓ Be consistent.
✓ Provide Superior Customer Service (like no other company).

How will I Build Brand Loyalty?

Branding Tip:

Always Be Branding

Step 15
Brand Partnerships

Step 15 is creating strategic brand partnerships. A partnership is important but is especially important when developing a brand. Partnerships allow you to connect with other individuals and brands. Also, usually, small businesses and startups have limited funds for advertising and promotion; therefore, developing strategic partnerships is vital.

Take the next 30 minutes and Research Business Partnerships …

Apple and MasterCard just created a strategic partnership.

Strategic partnerships are not like a regular partnership where you find someone or something you like, and you decide to work together. A strategic partnership is where careful considerations are made so that the partnership is mutually beneficial.

By collaborating with an already established brand, you get to raise your brand's awareness, but for you to establish this type of partnership, your brand has to be one that the already established brand sees as an asset. Also, if you are bringing something new, edgy, and innovative to the market and have a great business plan in place, building these partnerships are not very hard. The parent company mainly wants to know how your brand can bring funds to their company.

Make a list of companies you want to collaborate with and why:

1. _____
2. _____
3. _____

Next, find out whom you need to contact.

Then start the conversation immediately (send email/DMs, etc.).

Create a partnership agreement that is mutually beneficial.

How will I develop strategic partnerships and with whom?

USE THIS AREA TO WRITE
ABOUT YOUR BRAND

_____

_____

_____

_____

_____

_____

_____

_____

_____

_____

_____

Step 16
Brand's Website

Step 16 is creating or revamping your brand's website. A website is very important, and you should have one if you have a business and you are trying to create a powerhouse brand. Sure, social media accounts are great, but a website is needed to solidify you and your brand as solid.

Take the next 30 minutes and Research why websites are Important...

If someone is not willing to invest in a domain name and a professional website, it is very unlikely that they are willing to invest in building their brand and consumers can see this. If you already have a website, we will review the checklist to help ensure your website is cohesive and represents the brand. However, if you do not have a website, now is the time to get one if you want to be looked upon as a real brand.

If you can afford to hire someone to create your website, that is great, but if you cannot, you can create your website on sites like:

✓ Squarespace.
✓ Wix.
✓ WordPress.

When creating the content for your brand's website, make sure:

✓ The information is in the brand's voice and consistent.
✓ How your company solves a problem is apparent.
✓ The colors and graphics represent the brand.
✓ It is visually appealing and highlights the brand.
✓ It is Mobile Friendly.
✓ It has all of the brand's contact information.

Do I have a Brand Website? If so, does it represent the Brand? If not, create one today!

USE THIS AREA TO WRITE
ABOUT YOUR BRAND

_____

_____

_____

_____

_____

_____

_____

_____

_____

_____

_____

_____

_____

_____

_____

_____

_____

_____

_____

_____

_____

_____

_____

_____

Step 17
Networking

Step 17 is identifying organizations; you can join to create your network.

Take the next 30 minutes and Research organizations you can join…

Joining organizations that are associated with the type of brand you are building is very important for the following reasons.

You get to:

- ✓ Network with like-minded individuals.
- ✓ Develop Leadership Skills.
- ✓ Learn from others in your field.
- ✓ Build your Brand's awareness.
- ✓ Build your resume and reputation in the field.
- ✓ Remain motivated and inspired.
- ✓ Possibly find Strategic Partnerships.
- ✓ Solidify yourself and your brand as a philanthropic company.

If you own a printing company there are printing associations for example:

- ✓ Printing Industry Association of Georgia Incorporated.
- ✓ Printing Communications Association.

If you own an event planning company, there are event-planning associations. For example:

- ✓ Event planning association.
- ✓ Associations and Organizations for Event Planners.

What are some associations or organizations you can join?

1. _____
2. _____
3. _____

What Associations will I Join?

USE THIS AREA TO WRITE
ABOUT YOUR BRAND

_____

_____

_____

_____

_____

_____

_____

_____

_____

_____

_____

_____

_____

Step 18
Brand Promotion

Step 18 is promoting the brand by putting your company's information/logo on products. Personalizing items is important for a new brand because it is very cost effective and is an easy way to market.

Take the next 30 minutes and Research Promo items …

Brand Promotion is also important because it allows the brand to be marketed through multiple people and multiple channels because anyone who has the merchandise with the logo or slogan on it is now a marketer of your brand for no cost other than the expense of the item. Creating promotional products can be very fun with the many items that you can add your logo too, but should represent the brand, so choose wisely. Products that are commonly used for merchandising are:

- ✓ Apparel (T-shirts/Hats).
- ✓ Pens/Notebooks.
- ✓ Refrigerator magnets.
- ✓ Key Chains.
- ✓ Magnets.

However, innovative items you can utilize to brand merchandise are:

- ✓ Junk Drives.
- ✓ Water Bottles.
- ✓ Mouse Pads.
- ✓ Candy/Snacks.
- ✓ Umbrellas.

Companies like; Vista Print, Café Press, & Custom Ink makes it very affordable and accessible for everyone to properly promote. All you need is a logo and maybe your slogan. I would add my website and any hashtags that are associated with your brand.

What Promotional Items will I utilize?

USE THIS AREA TO WRITE
ABOUT YOUR BRAND

_____

_____

_____

_____

_____

_____

_____

_____

_____

_____

_____

_____

_____

Step 19
Branding Events

Step 19 is creating branding events. No other form of branding and marketing can cover more ground than hosting an event. Having events is an effective way to build your brand because you can plan and execute it exactly how you like and communicate with your audience exactly how you like in your brand's voice.

Take the next 30 minutes and Research Promotional Events...

Companies have product launches, holiday parties, community events, and even birthday parties to assist with brand building. Also, having a brand event is much more than putting your logo on napkins and creating invitations.

The event should have a purpose, be strategically organized, and marketed effortlessly.

The food and decorations should:
- ✓ Be consistent with the brand's theme.
- ✓ Have the colors of the logo and company.
- ✓ Compliment the company.

These events should be marketed via:
- ✓ Social Media.
- ✓ Flyers.
- ✓ Word of mouth.

Additionally if needed, you can hire an event planner. Remember you are using this event as a brand builder. Therefore, more consideration is required.

Start planning a Branding Event Today!

USE THIS AREA TO WRITE
ABOUT YOUR BRAND

_____

_____

_____

_____

_____

_____

_____

_____

_____

_____

_____

Step 20
Social Media

Step 20 is ensuring you have a presence on social media.

There used to be a time where you could successfully build a brand without ever having to do anything behind a computer except maybe send a few emails. Traditional marketing is still relevant, but the fastest way to build a brand in this day in age is through social media.

Take the next 30 minutes and Research Successful Social Media Trends …

I have personally seen individuals who own new brands and within a year or two are instantly famous with grandeur brands because of their activities on social media.

Social Media sites include but are not limited to:
- ✓ Instagram.
- ✓ Facebook.
- ✓ Twitter.
- ✓ Snapchat.
- ✓ Linkedin.
- ✓ Pinterest.
- ✓ And a few more.

Social media sites allow you to reach a mass amount of people with one click and are ultimately the fastest way to build a brand today. Social media allows you to provide your consumer with what the brand is doing and saying instantly. Content can be created or purchased. You can use platforms like Hootsuite or Planoly to schedule posts and make sure your posts:
- ✓ Are aligned with your brand's voice.
- ✓ Are professional.
- ✓ Are consistent. (Post at least once a day)

Create a Social Media posting Schedule.

Social Media Posting Example:

	Facebook	Twitter	LinkedIn	Pinterest	Google+
Minimum	3 X per week	5 X per week	2 X per week	5 X per day	3 X per week
Maximum	10 X per week	none	5 X per week	10 X per day	10 X per week

USE THIS AREA TO WRITE
ABOUT YOUR BRAND

Step 21
Brand Consistency

Step 21 is the final and most vital component of building your brand, and this is remaining consistent. The Consistency of the brand has to carry over in the:

- ✓ Marketing.
- ✓ Messaging.
- ✓ Content.
- ✓ Events.
- ✓ And everything associated with the brand.

To keep your brand consistent; make sure everything has the same voice, look, and all represent the company. Brand consistency builds brand trust and the messaging through all funnels should be the same. You should not be saying nor doing one thing on Instagram and then something else on Facebook. If an email is sent out and a flyer is designed for the same event, everything should look the same, the wording should be consistent, and those who come in contact with anything your brand puts out will know it is from your company.

Ways to ensure consistency across the brand is to:

- ✓ Have a constant use of the logo.
- ✓ The slogan if applicable.
- ✓ The brand's color and all messaging through all the communication channels should be the same.

Consistent brands become recognizable brands, and recognizable brands become powerhouse brands. Powerhouse Brands have customer demand and customer loyalty and ultimately achieves longevity and financial success.

How will I ensure brand consistency?

USE THIS AREA TO WRITE
ABOUT YOUR BRAND

_____

_____

_____

_____

_____

_____

_____

_____

_____

_____

_____

Step 22
Bonus Day
Brand's Logo

Step 22 is the single most important thing to do and have for your brand, which is your brand's logo. Your brand's message is your company's voice, and your brand's logo is the face of your company and will be the one thing that consumers will think about when they think of your brand.

When we think of McDonald's, we automatically think of the:
- ✓ Yellow Arch.

When we think of Nike, we think of the:
- ✓ Check or Swoosh.

Also, when we think of Starbucks despite if you are a coffee drinker or not, we think of that green logo, which for years individuals have been baffled about trying to figure out the meaning of it. Research indicates that the Starbucks logo represents a seductive and irresistible quality, which is what the coffee stands for. Despite not knowing what the Starbuck's logo really means, it is successful because it is stamped in the minds of its consumers. Making Starbucks the largest coffee retailer in the world with over 15,000 stores in over 42 countries.

Logos should:
- ✓ Be Unique;
- ✓ Represent the Brand;
- ✓ Have a Purpose;
- ✓ Memorable; and
- ✓ Professionally designed.

Now answer what does my logo say about my brand?

Letter from the Author:

Congratulations on completing this 21 step guide to assist with building your brand. I commend you for making the first steps and working diligently to getting to this point. As a business consultant/coach for almost two decades, I have seen over the years that the hardest part of building a brand is understanding how brands are perceived. Many people think that building a brand is creating a logo and a website, but as you can see from the 21 steps, it takes much more than that, which is why I decided to put together this guide to assist you with the process. Completing this book and all the necessary steps is just the beginning of the brand building journey. Use this guide as a resource even after you have completed your 21 steps. Always remember to brand often and brand with a purpose.

Thanks.
Dr. Synovia Dover-Harris

Contact Info
Dr.Synovia@A2ZBookspublishing.com
Facebook/Synovia Dover-Harris
Instagram @Dr.Synovia

Order online at amazon.com and all other online distributors

Also Available:

Ready Set Write your Book
Ready Set Launch your Business

Coming Soon:-

Ready Set Launch your Private Label
Ready Set Build your Team

Interested in Writing and or Publishing a BOOK???

Visit: www.A2ZBooksPublishing.com

www.ingramcontent.com/pod-product-compliance
Lightning Source LLC
Chambersburg PA
CBHW031904200326
41597CB00012B/533